Doctor of None

N.R.K. Hoffman

BookLeaf
Publishing

Presentation by *BookLeaf Publishing*

Web: www.bookleafpub.com

E-mail: info@bookleafpub.com

ISBN: 9789395755023

First edition 2022

DEDICATION

For my family.

ACKNOWLEDGEMENT

Never underestimate the power of an active listener. Thank you to all who listen to me, and thank you to all who have trusted me enough to share, and allowed me to listen. My family, my friends in Kansas City, London, and everywhere else, thank you for being there when I needed you.

My love of poetry is inspired by the following wordsmiths: Carol Ann Duffy, Taylor Swift, The 1975, William Shakespeare, Linkin Park, William Ernest Henley, The Brontë Sisters, and Julia Donaldson.

PREFACE

When I googled what to write for a book's preface, my results told me to share the book's origin story and outline my motivation and inspiration for writing the book.
The driving force behind this book came down to two things; algorithms and denial.

In a condensed and rigorous graduate program, I was devastated to be verging on my third "C" grade. The curriculum for my Doctorate of Physical Therapy permitted only two "C" grades throughout the two-and-a-half-years of the program. Despite losing hours and hours of my life poring over my curriculum and trying my hardest to make it through, I was faced with the dread of crushing failure despite all my tireless work. With my future PT career hanging in the balance, I did what any aspiring writer would do and started searching "Free professional writing programs" and "How to successfully self-publish a book."

On one tab of my browser, I populated my recent search history with "get rich quick" style buzz phrases related to publishing a novel.

How wonderful, I thought, I'm going to become a famous author! And it never would have happened if I didn't suck at PT school. Wouldn't that have made my failures seem charmingly destined and my story, ordained?

On a separate browser tab, I simultaneously prodded different phrases into the keyboard. "Physical Therapy Assistant salary" and "Anatomy tutor."
I'm not the first one to have an unforeseen crossroads parse out the optimist and realist within me, but there I was; a torn, frustrated, living dichotomy. I swore internally that I'd get extra experience, that I'd nail my future classes, and that I'd absolutely never give up on getting my doctorate because that would be weak. At the same time I was planning steps of how I could become a successfully published author within a year. I'd prove that I was valuable and talented in some kind of way, and I'd pick up my doctorate in physical therapy anyway. I had the idea that all the threads of my paths would be weaved together cohesively and surely I'd be smart enough to do it all, and do it quickly. Surely.

Had I opened my mind wider, I would have understood that a change in course would have been a good choice for me. I might have realized that diversifying my existing skills and finding work in other fields, didn't mean I couldn't complete a doctorate. Had I looked up possible vacations to give my mind a breather, or delved into family-friendly careers in writing, I probably wouldn't have found targeted ads to a site that published your own little book of poetry. Like I said; algorithms and denial.

I don't need to include a qualifying statement along with my enthusiasm for sharing this book, but I feel that I want to. I understand that this book is likely to only be seen by my friends and family but that doesn't mean I'm any less excited to share it.
The first reason is because poetry is one of the rawest forms of self-revelation, and who better to reveal your full self to, than the ones who already love you. The second reason I'm excited to share this book is because it symbolizes turning my attention to the valuable things in this life; my family, my friends, my passions and things that make me present, connected, and good. I believe writing is one of those things, and as I switch to taking just a few of my classes for school this year, but having the privilege to work as a full-time copywriter, I'm excited to

spread my writing wings once more and
eventually publish more than a poetry book.

Mum, Dad, Jake, and my wonderful in-laws, I'm
good! You always knew I had spice in me,
poetry is just a way of channeling it into words,
so don't be alarmed. Ryan, you are no stranger to
my melodrama so all I have to say is thank you
for listening to it again, and thank you for loving
me.

In The Beginning

I sit here leaking - like the drip of a tap.
My brother listens to Linkin Park.
I'm craving the soak of the rain on my skin
And I'm thirsty for rage in the dark.

Chasing wishes that taste like whispers
My fingertips tear up my brow.
Grasping at grass, that's thinner than straws
I question my why and my how.

I curse my name for steeping in shame,
I scratch these words into my skull:
"You're lucky, you're fine, you senseless bitch"
Yet I'm aching, hollow, and dull.

For the second time in my short life
I'm stricken with failure to launch.
The malady of privilege etched in my bones
Despite resolution so steadfast and staunch.

Climbing the ladder, I splintered my palms.
Hoisting dense hope and ambition.
Each rung closer - My peak and their pride.
Vengeful illness tamed in remission.

Hateful gravity takes no mind,

In mocking the blood on my hand.
Knocked down. Despair. My route - disrepair
No stranger to this strange, ruined land.

But this time I tried. I swore it was better.
No martyr. My struggles were spoken.
Now an old wooden puppet collapsed on the
floor,
My strings have been slashed and broken.

Bones have failed me, my eyes search high
There's no ascendency in my path now.
There's no step-up… but I will step forward.
I release my nails from my brow.

The unrequited love of hunting a passion,
Is a cupidic arrow to the heel,
Wedged in flesh to course through our blood
In feverous dreams, only self they reveal.

Yet it is honest like only true love can be,
A motive - reckless and pure.
It's right. So I'll write. Right here and right now.
While my brother blasts rock through the door.

I Don't

They all say: "You got this!"
It hands me no hope.
It's just cheers from the sidelines
They don't cast any rope.

'Cos in swampland, I'm drowning
There's one shattered wreck
With no surface to lever
My weight onto the deck.

My nails are blood
Clawing splinters off the boat.
But they all say "You got this!"
Well what if I don't.

What a western dream.
You go forth with resilience,
And trudging through trenches
Will in time reveal brilliance.

Just keep going. I swear
It's endurance that matters
But that doesn't seem right
When I'm shredded to tatters.

If I'm a shadow of self-worth
Squandering family and friends,
How can they say
It's all worth it in the end?

And when the lines in my face
show more than meridians.
I don't wanna be trapped
by American idioms.

Leg up. Or luck's up.
But don't give up. I don't.
I beg the battle grants survival
I surrender when it won't.

Doctor of None

I dress then stress. Dilemma. Distress,
No glimmer I find, at all.
A trajectory, failed. My drive - impaled.
Unable to balance the ball.

With patience, gifted. Patients lifted,
Eye to eye. Contact. Support.
She established connection but under inspection
A competency that questioned proport.

I hold an old hand, caress wrinkled skin.
My work here has just begun.
But with struggled performance, my appeal turns
dormant.
A master of relation but a doctor of none.

A healthy child, good-natured and mild,
Soon he hits. Target. Trouble.
Proceeding with kindness, her intent - a
blindness
A toy sword bursting the bubble.

Love him. Harder. I can't be a martyr.
Marking the divergence of my son.
Write a letter, to swear it gets better.

A master of belief but a doctor of none.

Home. Sweet house. No reason to grouse,
Privileged for luxury and chance.
Oak bookcases, tall. Cursive signs on the wall.
Each space to enjoy and enhance.

But Pinterest tricks and throw pillows won't fix,
Boundless chores that remain undone.
In a state of perpetual moving, no promise is
soothing
I'm a master of ideas but a doctor of none.

Girls will be girls. They fill up your world
With obsession, and doting that's resplendent
Reciprocate quickly, and tie the bonds thickly.
No care to a carved codependence.

When a flame catches kindling, the embers are
left dwindling
When it burns as fierce as the sun.
Friendships sit deep, but with too many to keep
I'm a master of connection but a doctor of none.

She jumped to cross oceans, predisposed with
the notion
Of devotion. And binding. The vow.
Of visceral tenacity, determined capacity.
To give and forgive anyhow.

But promise turns sour, in the 25th hour
My vision fades and my family are gone.
Hard to be a romantic when my mind has turned
frantic.
I'm a master of will but a doctor of none.

Smart. Well-rounded. Knowledge, compounded.
A grey tile for a storm cloud mosaic.
But from outside the box, when a strong will
knocks
A young mind is marked difficult and archaic.

One teacher alone sought the capability I
brought,
An inquiring brain with battles unwon.
But one teacher isn't enough, when self-worth is
scuffed.
A master of potential but a doctor of none.

Snap. Each time. Experiences of mine,
Are just snapshots yet drawn in black ink
I'm ceasing the change, from an aim that's
deranged
Resolute. Though I know will think

Of school parts missed, the nearly-right boys
kissed.
A pattern that ancient history begun.

Never quite enough, never gets less rough
I'm a master of chance but a doctor of none.

Do It

Pursue it
Do it
I'll go through it
This time I won't be told
I waited
Blew it

Smashed the bullseye
Pierced right through it
Don't stop
Keep up
Phew! I knew it

It's a farce
I know
But I can't undo it
No choice but now
So screw it
I'll do it

White noise
Screeches
No care to it
Buckle down
Review it. Redo it.

Consequences
Confirmed
I'll ensue it
Take no leave
Debut it. Do it.

Mark it on your soul
Scratch
Tattoo it
Don't be the one
Who overthrew it
Wear it like identity
Don't subdue it
The dream
Yourself
Are One
So do it

Headstrong. True.
How they'll view it
Magic erased
So I redrew it
Nurtured
Housed
Yes. I regrew it
Provided
Now I'll dive into it.

The Carol Of The Seasons

On iridescent path of flattened leaf
I crush, and crush the rain beneath.
The sun that touches the campus, clear,
Shan't touch the ground that's settled here.

My thoughts are the mud, steeped, like tea.
They mock the warmth in parody.
While sunlight brings a brighter birth,
Blossom has fallen, kissing the earth.

Birds of a feather decorate the lake.
The fall of a branch. A Crash. A Break.
In a blink, gone. In my head then,
A vow to return complete, again.

Winds change, and I grasp a chance
To use their rhythm and start to dance.
The woodland thickens, adorning a scene
Of dreams and challenge, painted green.

The forest calls. Breath of air.
Exploring nature, I stand and swear
That peace will be where it's grown and planted.
Nurtured. Surviving our storms, if granted.

As leaves drop, the campus is colder.
A sign understood - I'm now a bit older.
Green fades to orange. Unsettling breeze,
But suddenly the path has cleared through the
trees.

The ground glistens like birthday cake,
Silent walkers. A frosted lake.
The backdrop whispers "You will be fine."
If trees keep blooming and the sun will shine.

On iridescent path, the buds unravel
A road that beckons new souls to travel.
Forever it stays, forever it will be
While we vow to save it, like it saved we.

A Day In The Life

A day in the life
Beautiful boys in each hand
Corn on the cob for last minute dinner plans.

A Diaper that smells like a nuclear bomb,
Eager eyes
Fish that are neon to feed in the pond

German classical on google
Hair knotted in places
Ice that freezes my teeth and drips down little
faces.

Letter J homework
Kisses on dog noses and brothers
Legs that find companions under the covers.

Mug for mothers day, coffee rich and ready
Nachos for lunch
Octopus is new favorite teddy.

Peas in a pod keychains, attached to a label.
Rainbows in suburbia as water fills the play
table.

Snow cones, slip down syrupy chins
Two hooded bath towels expose four shiny
shins.

Udemy course tabs, opened from a list
"Very Good!" S exclaims with his hot dog in
fist.

Walks at lunch, with ears that are floppy
X's cross out homework mistakes
Yogurt is sloppy.

Z loves having hair brushed every night.

This is all water.
A day in the life.

The Scent Of Books

Books release whiffs of dust when dropped.
The scent of academia pungent like the wood
Of a forest, that the tales invite.

Buried in pathways are pages
Igniting a new personality when one is needed.
Silence is golden. Goldleaf. Molten candle
Whispers to stay longer.

Knowledge flickers then suddenly brightens
Fueled by the food of yearning
For learning enlightens a child and adult alike.

There's no telling what one will find. One more
chapter.
Sparking truth in olden times. Gold mine.
Hold it. Mine to share.

Take yours. Served freely are the laws of
Nature and narratives of healing.
Dare for feeling and new believing.

Penny for your soul. It could take it all,
The dust envelops and molds you like clay

A potter's thumbs merging the two creating a
unified entity

Architects have formed the walls of stories,
A vast cathedral of standing glory that ascertains
sanctuary.
For all refugees of life begun.

Asylum is sought. Found in education
Yet it seems the meritocracy - a hypocrisy of
fading dreams
Begs question of paving the steps of ascendency.

In another, innovation torches the way.
Tarnished nations in disarray, motivate others to
 Pay and be paid. Watch how it's swept
underneath
To mold into a brick that builds a pyramid of
clay.

Unheeded

I look at my friends through a mask or a veil
It's nice to have known you
When I'm gone, tell me what will prevail?
A weak link plucked from a paper chain.

I'm really sorry to hear about your divorce
I said to my friend once.
As I was really sorry to hear about his divorce.
A barometer sensed the change in atmosphere
Splutters and grimaces
What the hell was she thinking?
You don't tell someone you're sorry to hear
about their divorce
When you want to tell someone you're sorry to
hear about their divorce.

Wow you just come right out with it don't you.

Not a word. Not one. That I could tell.
Was offered when a part of my world crumbled
to hell.
Two weeks ago.
Hi. One friend said. How are you doing today?
And he met my eyes with every word.

As if he were asking
How are you doing today?
Fine. I said. How are you?

But people will be there
And that might be all we can hope
That they're there. Their presence, a present.
That they won't be scared. Of contagious bad
luck.
Failing friends.
They say "We'll still hang out! - Don't worry"
But they're not telling me.
They don't realize that yet.

Hugs and shots. A friend comes to hang at my
house.
She stays a while. She says she'll come back.
I think she will.
This is her language now.
People don't like words.
Better to communicate unspoken, unheard.
No sticks and stones
But no call on the phone.
Silence can never not hurt me.

Everyone thinks they're different.
But if I seem like the only one who draws hugs
with confessions

Paints friendships from secrets
And holds hands with deep conversation.
Maybe my recipe is broken.
Is there nothing worse?
They think.
The wrong thing.
I didn't want to make my words sting.
I don't know what to say.
So it's definitely best to keep words locked
away.

Or maybe
I'm sorry about to hear about school, Nadia.
We're really going to miss you next year.
Is all I needed.
To know they're sorry to hear about school
And they're going to miss me next year.
No care impeded.
Wherever I am, I matter.
Message heeded.

Doll

Your voice sounded like a warm cup of tea
Like David Attenborough
Recommending books to read.

When your wife died
I think I brought hope
At least that's how you looked at me whenever
we spoke.

You would stroke my hair
And call me doll

Now I'm trying playing tug of war with my soul

Trying to tease the words out
If you deserve them.
Memories fade to sepia
I endeavour to preserve them.

You wouldn't see us.
We couldn't even stop by.
I thought grudges crumble
When you're ready to die.

But you didn't care. What did I mean
To you. If you left the scene
Before it was over
And now my son has never seen
You. He won't know your face
And why. Does that make me feel disgrace
Should I have stormed into your place
When you were ill? and given you grace
That you didn't know what was happening, mind
displaced.
And now my love and fury are interlaced
Latching on to something, unerased.
As now there's no curtain call, no trace
You had a role to fill, you've been replaced.
Understudy. Understand, I've studied your face
But my children will never know your adoring
embrace.
And yet they don't need help to fill this space

… But boy, how I wish they did.

So they will never know you. I'm glad I did.
A pretty park, a large hand.
A redheaded kid.

Another you would've wanted
The story to change.
Holidays all together.
Center stage.

Betrayed by your life,
Puppet master, with wings.
Which let you feel slighted
While pulling the strings.
My offences were unconscious
But you were conditional.
Muddy misdeeds
That were somewhat volitional.

I could have reached out more
I was too carefully treading.
Did you really care that much,
About the food at my wedding?
I know there was more
That you clasped in your heart
You could never tell me,
So I thought I'd start.

I think we were lucky,
We shared and connected.
With love and expectation
Simultaneously infected.

Loving you hurt, so I know you existed.
Embedded memories
Joyful. Gifted.

Don't regret when I say

You've left such a deep hole
I'll think of the times that
That you called me doll.

And told me you loved me.
And drunk wine in Spain,
Chuckling in the moonlight
While speaking my name.

Sanity

Searching inspiration afar, around
But I don't know what I shall do if it's found.

Tied up and muddy, messy and sore,
Navigating my way through a tunnel shielded by
your own shit and gore.

Blindsided spectacular and oracle of slight
Punching through the rushes and falling in
plight.

You're raising yourself to a standard but instead
of pulling me up,
You'd skip three rungs on the ladder looking
down to ensure I can't catch up.

We created a man-cave with decorative pillows,
Boulders up, you dug further. Space between us
billows.

Peel off like a scab, still committed to healing.
Please give me space, I should tell you how I'm
feeling.

Sailing to different islands bent on creating route,
I try climb aboard but my company, mute.

Wonky and slowly I send you a smile,
Swollen debilitation underneath all the while.

Clawing you lovingly, of you I'm aware
You're disgusted, determined that I didn't care.

Go far I don't need you... except for it all.
Abandoned. Watch me away, I'll scatter and crawl.

Location to location, connected like stars.
Exploring the earth while you hide out on Mars.

I know you so well yet don't know you at all.
Behind the veil you glimmer. Wind. And Rock Wall.

Knight. Castle. Sword. Sheath.
Admiring your senses, stargazing beneath.

Alas my evasive one, removed, tenacious.
Faked your own life and accused me of loquacious
Straight honesty is all - But by fuck I'm ungracious

Unimpressed as you reveal your spite and
veracious

Unfiltered you ask. Unchecked you desire
Unequipped to handle questions you might
inspire.

Because I'm adoring and complicated.
Heartbeat. Brain.
Expecting my silence. Inflicting me pain.

I'll listen and breath. But I can't be a machine
It's okay you say whilst ripping marriage at
seam.

Not perfect. Here's my gift - Our love that's
spacious,
Laughing in the shadows wrapped in nights of
salacious.
Then you tell me you need a path that's
audacious.
What the fuck? I'm a fucking light and
vivacious

It's easy. Forever. Webbed dreams and laugh.
I stick us together, you cut me in half.

Creeping. Streetlights. Horizon run.
You fuck me like this and baby, I'm done

Today. Won't end. Knives jagger and thine
You sleep on your back, I massage your spine.

You broke me. Satiated a soul with a lie.
Driving our train to the pier. And bye.

My fault. My flight. Straight con till morning.
Second to the left at small promise's dawning.

Won't shout. Won't sleep Remember the
tightness. In chest.
Better our lives. Rock souls. Please leave out all
the rest.

Julietta

Sometimes I wish i could be
Not me.
Not someone I know,
Not someone I've seen

Just a girl
An image
A snapshot of peace.

Julietta
We'll call her
Freckled and fair
She wears a blue ribbon
In her long curly hair.

She lives in rural France
Today, but it could be any
Because Julietta's town
Has no need for media, hi-tech stuff,
Or chastising screens showing children they're
not enough.

They laugh at the frivolity of it
While sipping their lunchtime wine
The bread is fresh

And so is the breeze
Cotton skirts that flirt at the knees.

Julietta doesn't bake
Well she does (she's French)
But that would be too obvious
She's a florist
Or a therapist
She studied in a big school,
She left her town
As young people are always obligated to.

Julietta is smart,
She rolled her eyes
At people's need for big dreams
And grass greener lies.

But she did what she must
Knowing they'd hardly relent
The village
Their love
Their hold
They'd never stop nagging if she stewed
Never forgive her if she she didn't return
So Julietta obediently left to find something to
learn.

A love affair or two
A professor who saw

The pressure of talent knocking at her door.
But three years was enough.
To see what she could be,
Contently leaving her big world trajectory

Now she has friends
Food
Family
The scent of lavender at the stream
Moss paths, trees
Branches that weave around undisturbed beams.

So there she sits
A big table and laughter
Finches that make nests in the wooden rafter.
A full life
But a simple dream
Existence is pencil drawing
Etched in reverie.

Life tastes like the wine Julietta drinks
It's local, familiar, sweet and rich.
It's the best she's ever had
The best wine in Southern France
Many people have said.
But I wonder if just sometimes she craves a beer
instead.

Does Julietta steep?

Does Julietta cry?
Is Julietta that different from you and I
What if she took the job in Paris?
Let the modern flat with the chrome
Didn't leave it all for her mother and a nice boy,
at home.
What if she grabbed the man that made her legs
weak
And kissed him
It's not something she speaks of
And if she cared, you'd never know
She's content, surrounded
By a life where she matters - that's sustainable,
grounded.

She's the opposite of me.
But also the same
A blessed and complicated life
By a different name.

Work-Life

I'm not your perfect candidate,
None of us are, indeed.
I just happened to match the correct answer
As to why I'm what you need.
Neither of us need one another
In order to succeed.
I'll order my stationary from your credit card.
And find just the right level of greed.

It's not your fault or anyone's
White collar noise that makes no sound.
You're breeding a culture
In a petri dish.
Embedded and abound.
But I'll have Fridays off early so at least I'll be
around.

I'll tell you I'm organized
And thrive on collaboration and winning.
Just to look out the window
To the seeds of the sycamore spinning
To the ground.
I'm just doing what the middle class does.

I'm thankful to be here

And maintain your gaze for one second more
than I should
Enough that you think about it
And reckon
That we would, if I could.
I'm just doing what all women do.

Let me be home
And weave my way out of the city
Just to lie on my bed in self-pity
Scrolling through my phone
I'm just doing what young people do.

I see their pink faces
And that's what all this is for.
The shine in their eyes as they see me arrive
One hour sooner than ever before
I'm just doing what all mothers do.

I'm distant tonight
And maybe you're not the instigator
So I'll tell you I love you
While staring at my hands as
they use a magnet to hold your mail
On the door of the refrigerator.
I'm just doing what all wives do.

Road after road,
It's troubles that maim my affection,

But I bought us all a trip on a plane
And I've experience with deflection
So I watch my kids dance in the water
In Spain
We're afloat
As I check my email on remote.
I'm just doing what we're all here to do.

A Storybook For Shia & Zevi

In a big, big hospital
On a silent floor,
A nurse holding a baby
Walks through the door.

She hands him to Mummy,
Who filled up with joy.
To be happily holding
Her first little boy.

Daddy was hungry
And Mummy was tired
But our baby was a gift
So we named him Shia.

The world is big
And Shia was small
So nobody noticed a new baby,
In Greece or Nepal.

But for some people that morning;
Their world was changed.
They had a new person to love
And here are their names:

Mummy, Daddy and Siri
And Gigi and Papa,
There was Mommom and Pop
And Dinky and Saba.

Your Great Grandpas, Robert and David
And Nana gave a huge smile!
So did Bob, Donna, Auntie Lana
And your uncles Jake, Justin and Kyle.

Your Great Aunts and Uncles
And cousins and friends too.
Their lives filled with happiness
Because of you.

You grew up funny
You grew up smart.
You grew up talented
In reading, numbers and art.

We thought we were busy,
Raising our super son.
But then the universe said,
"Well you can't have just one!"

So in another hospital bed,
Sat the same tired Mummy,
Who had another little boy
Taken out of her tummy.

He had a dimple in his cheek,
He was a little more heavy -
A cuddly little wolf.
So we called him Zevi.

The world is old
And Zevi was new
So nobody noticed a baby
In France or Peru.

But for some people that morning,
Their world was changed.
They had a new person to love
And here are their names:

Mum, Dad, Shia and Siri
And Dinky and Saba.
There was Mommom and Pop
And Gigi and Papa.

Great Grandpas Robert and David
Nana, Bob and Donna too,
And your Aunties Megan and Alanna
Cheered with joy for you!

Your Uncles Jake, Justin and Kyle
Great Uncles and Aunts as well
With cousins and friends

All put under a spell.

Because when you joined us
The world was strange,
But your smiles and snuggles
Made a beautiful change.

You're growing up up loving
And you're growing up funny
Talented in making friends,
And music and running.

So to Shia and Zevi,
You have to remember.
Our family is perfect
Because of our two newest members.

From the very first day
Each of you brought joy
You are our most favorite
Smiling boys.

The universe is big
And our decisions are small
But if you make good ones
They can change us all.

We'll adore you forever
You're all we need in the world

(But convince your Daddy
If you want a baby girl!)

Blazing Haven (A Writer's Way)

In ocean azure, I find my brain
A rhythm of freedom so beautifully insane.

The roots of the wood, creep up my soul
Holding viscerally until words roll.

Clear as the dark in piercing night
Path like the thread of a lighthouse light.

If bricks build walls, then also a home
A segment of suffering that is finally owned.

Lugubrious manor grows but won't haunt us,
Housing a woman who's novel and dauntless.

Backward and benevolent is a tiny town,
Diamonds of ice on branches sinking them
down.

A harmony of femininity plays a revolution,
A champion of obstacles that mask the solution.

A love almost forgotten, a war-torn stage
Bleeds out words of revelation onto a page.

In crushing solace, death opens a door
To converse with the men she's loved before.

With power is sacrifice they prepare a blade
Of grass, or a knife. A plan is laid.

A faith might be killed, but soon reborn
As courage bred from ash and scorn.

Aiden

[The poem, "Aiden," is in memory of the victims of needless gun violence; the ones that were killed and the ones left behind]

They trusted in our country
Like they trusted in that day.
Skinned away from their breath of life
What on earth would they have to say.

You'll grow up to learn of peace
And immediately understand violence.
You'll close your eyes and speak to them
But only ever receive their silence.

A heartbreak stronger than death streaks by
It pierces your every hour.
Nothing will ever make it right,
No money has that power.

She can never hold you close
Whisper you're everything and more.
She was robbed of her forever calling
The name she gave you, through the door.

She'll miss your interests, friends, and
milestones
Stolen are her words and lessons.
The right is not mine. But everything is wrong.
So I'll try and capture her essence.

She'd say "I adored you more than anything,
My heart is fused inside your chest.
Having you in my arms felt perfect
No-one has ever been more blessed."

"Feel me everywhere, take me with.
Please kindle every ember.
We loved you from the start, we stay till the end.
When it fades, Aiden, remember."

I have a son your age. He smiles a lot.
And sneaks toy cars into his bath
No single child in any world deserves to be
Orphaned at two and a half.

I can't promise my children a mightier world,
But I can promise I'll teach at length:
To cherish life and plant ruthless seeds
Of infallible compassion and strength.

If the anger infects and inflicts your mind
Try not to surrender to fear.
Let your family shield your pain,

Everyone's better for having you here.

I hope one day you read my words
I plead they grant respite of danger.
Some might bleed their blackness forth,
But there is love inside of strangers.

True Blood

You didn't embarrass me
But I'm embarrassed
By you,
By what you're saying.
How you're implying I should be embarrassed
Because I bleed
And bear children

As if that's something that's shameful.
Only you, seriously,
Only you could need us
To fill the world
With more fucking men.
Only to embarrass us when
Our bodies empty the blood
Needed to nurture your army -

How dare you.
How dare you insult me
Make a mockery of my brilliant body
And what it does
for you and the world.
And then tell me I'm sensitive
When you choose to insult me

And I raise my eyebrows
To you raising your voice.
And I'm the sensitive one,
Sure
Okay
Cunt.

Why does my blood scare you
When you shoot your guns and insist that
children
Be brought into the world
In a bloody mess.
Of the mothers who didn't want them
Who'll bleed in abuse
Or will bleed in neglect
Or will bleed in sickness.
Yet it's my giving blood
Non-violent and true
The only kind that's sacred
And that's what disgusts you.

The truth is in your manhood
Like the floppy elephant in the room
You're scared about my sex appeal
And what that means to you.
I'm a developed G-dess
Who's ready to bear
Fruits you'll never have
So I'd better beware.

If I have sex
I better get pregnant
That's what I deserve
For having female body parts
Or being ready for sex
Even if I'm not ready
Do I deserve it still?
Of course.
Bible folks have no fucking chill
Cos one woman once
Took fruit
And apparently that means we bleed
And are deserving of pain
So now my period
Is the reason for your fucked up brain.

A Deep, Hopeful Dark

There was never any plot
I made the bed
There's no striving for anything in life
Just starving in the head.

Crows caw. And caw. And caw. And caw.
Hitting like a migraine in the core
Feeling sure they'd transform into doves
And melodies of love, and more.

Wretched strain bleeds insane
There is nothing physical
But I can't take the pain.
It's all the same. It's never again
My loved ones are quizzical
I'm the only one. To blame.

I'm so sickly
Obsessed with victory
I grasp time slickly
Hickory Dickory
Yet I can't do anything quickly.
But simply find what makes me tick.
Tick. Tick.
Tock.

What's Up

I might finally know
Four little letters
A curse and a home.
The response when struggle asked the question.
Thud, went the answer
Boom - A suggestion.

It's been a part of me all along
I walk an empty street
But Greenday were wrong
It's full of dreams
The dark room is where
Life comes alive
And we don't need beams
To guide the night
My memories, pictures
That fade into light

And I ask how I'd feel
Without my disorder
A probably better, cherished daughter
Don't swear on my life
I only need me
I can promise nothing
As I internally speed
And dart
Chasing after cars

I thought were parked
Oh Look - A crash.
Tomorrow I'll start.

Blind my eyes to the color
Drawing outlines in black
Storyboard
Penciled draft
One day I'll be back
Nails into palms.
I build my friends out of clay
I can't promise to respond
But I swear that I'll stay
Sat deep in a chair
To redraw jagged lines
Desperately destitute
And ready to shine

Best

In dedication to the old folks,
I know you've waited
"Awful daughter!" Mum will say
And I'd keep you baited
Because it's so fun
Winding you up.
Like a sparkly yo-yo
Who bounces and comes back
No matter what I throw.
But in laughing at yourself
You taught me the ability
To throw dirt off the shoulder
And ground myself in humility
Mum and Dad;
An odd couple.
Sometimes overbearing and tough -
You were consistent and connected
And that was more than enough
To make me strong
And lucid,
Unapologetically decided
That I was okay
As long as I am provided
With just a a sprinkle of family
Who deeply care

And steadfast friends
Who are always there.
Tolerance was important
You didn't have to make rules
It was just obvious
In our home
That equality was cool
But without need for brainwashing
And personality upheaval
It's just what you absorb
When you live with good people
None of us born rich
But we were all born stable
Telling Jake and I
To elevate anyone
With all that we're able
To do for the world.
But crap - this has got
A little intense
I just wanted to write sweet poem -
But in my defence
I decided to go freeform
Let my sentiments
Roam truly
Mum don't fetch your red pen
If my English is quite unruly
It's a new genre.
Jon come and see
Your daughter's written us a poem

Although it's not my best
But honestly that's the most showing
Of why I'm thankful,
Why I'm hashtag blessed
You only cared that I cared
It never had to be best.
Well… the best is good
After all, we are Jews
And just above average
Doesn't make the best news
When you're sharing your gossip
Animating your vision
But embellishment never hurt
So I give you my permission.
In return just one ask
Get up, be bolder
Best book your flights
Extend your nights
I don't care that you're older.
We'll fly to you,
And you'll fly on back
Coffee and talks with mum,
Tea and walks with dad.
An era of peace
Is the utmost pleasure
I hand you my honesty
And I hope it's a measure
Of how I've learned to respect you
Yes, yes I know

It wasn't always the case
But here I still stand
In a messy, happy place.
I'm full of pride
I'm full of content
The best time had
Is any time spent.

Igne Natura

By the hair of the dog
Or the will-o-the-wisps,
I unsheathe my dagger
And pierce through the mist.

Reviving offence, I care not
If plans gang aft agley,
An enemy horn sounds conquest bourne
While their branches solemnly sway.

The ebony night,
the equalizer of all
Drapes over the forest
Like a widow's shawl.

No cover hides,
My crown of fire
They turn to behold
As I charge through the mire.

Through spear, through shield
I carve through the mass.
A body, just flesh.
This too shall pass.

Our fight matters not
We are but one hoard.
I am the master of my fate.
Within the hands of the Lord.

I rise in resilience
Exalted and sure.
The path is dreaded
The heart is pure.

Nature clasps champion
Upon this beaten track.
Draw your quill to victory, friends.
Haste ye back soon. Haste ye back.